The **Origins** *of* **Tragedy**

& other poems

OTHER BOOKS BY KENNETH ROSEN

Whole Horse (1973)
Black Leaves (1980)
The Hebrew Lion (1989)
Longfellow Square (1991)
Reptile Mind (1993)
No Snake, No Paradise (1996)

The Origins *of* Tragedy

& other poems

KENNETH ROSEN

CavanKerry ⬧ Press LTD.

Library of Congress Cataloging-in-Publication Data

Rosen, Kenneth, 1940-
    The origins of tragedy, and other poems / by Kenneth Rosen.
        p. cm.
    ISBN 0-9707186-6-7
    I. Title.
PR3568.O768 O75 2002
811'.54--dc21   2002073710

Cover painting: *The Party* © 2001 by Richard Wilson, oil on
canvas, 16 in. x 21 in.

Cover and text design by Pamela Flint

First edition

CavanKerry Press Ltd.
Fort Lee, New Jersey
East Hampton, New York
www.cavankerrypress.com

for Patty Rosen
(SINE QUA NON)

Contents

I. Clear Dark Blue

II. All That Is Solid Melts into Air

III. Maps of Clamor

IV. A Portion for Foxes

V. A Spy Among Bacchae

The Origins of Tragedy

& other poems

I.
Clear Dark Blue
Clear Dark Blue

Morning star

evening star   salt of the sky
First the grave   dissolving into dawn

then the crucial   recrystallizing
from inmost depths   of clear dark blue

—James Merrill, "An Upward Look"

THE WOODS IN MARCH

Just the chevrons whitetail deer
Chew in the thin bark of young trees
Around the vernal equinox,
Snow in a state of surrender,
Melting into rivers and bottomless mud,
Evaporating up through its crust.
Something had to happen. A deer has to eat.
Often the young tree dies on its feet.
And the crystal ashes of moonlight
Melt like love in the languishing
Gaze of the aftermath, whose own
Unprotected nakedness gazes back,
Though blind and uncomprehending,
Pale and unable to say for sure:
> *I know you. You used to love me.*

FRIEND OF MY YOUTH

I wanted friendship to read like a book,
Totally engrossing, never ending, free
From the burden of my marooned,
Impenetrable condition of being. I'd nothing to offer
But limitless attention, and a hopeful, cheerful
Running commentary on virtually anything.
None of my friends could stand it
And deserted me in droves, especially you,
Sending your mother to the door
To say you weren't home, making
Whispered plans, and so on.

I couldn't play sports due to ignorance,
Paralysis, an inability to endure terrors
Of isolation in which one physical act
Determined the temporary status or stain
Whereby I was either a hero, outcast
Or nothing at all. Right field, right guard,
It was all a disaster. So when I at last left home,
I never went back. I suppose I could find out
Where you live, sit in my car across the street,
Watch your house with cravings as intense
As long ago. Perhaps after a few days

You'd notice and approach my vehicle, my face
Calm as a reptile's. I would say, "Here we are,
Sixty." Too late to see your children at about
The age we were when learning to take on the world

With greed, cunning, dishonesty and self-discipline,
To flutter from the branch, you to fly,
Me to fall, learn to crawl, spit, and bite
Venomously, which clearly wasn't enough,
Because one flicker of obtuse impatience
Across your face sends me back under the rock
And into the dark from which I've come.

THINKING OF KISSING YOU

Nothing was like it, nothing in itself to say
    Unless confirmed
With blunt serenity, *'It was nothing, please*
    Go away.' It was something
Like nothing, like a mistake which got
    As good as it gave,
So seemed like a lot, yet turned out to be not much,
    Though not for me, for whom
Something like nothing was like the moon certain nights,
    Stubborn, irregular, lingering
In eery nakedness, remembered unwillingly. Poor
    Moon, necessarily resentful,
Making a practice in life of simplicity, though both
    A huntress and priestess
Of solemn madness, protected by silence and ferocity,
    A band of friends, dogs, dim-witted
And murderous, who in glad frenzy believed I was a
    Stag. But I was Actaeon.
It was the forest. I saw you naked and I was lost.

THE BLACK FOREST

There are two voices in Brahms' 3rd *Symphony*,
    His and hers, Johannes and Clara's.
Robert was "away," having crippled his fingers
For musical tours with an elastic strap. He kept
Trying to drown himself in a half foot of water,
    Leaping off a footbridge into the Iser
And floundering like a cat hit by a car, like a carp
    Flopping in a rowboat. They allowed
    Him out of his cage again and again,
And to prove his genius he kept banging away
At the same tune with his damaged hands,
The melodic equivalent of 'Son-of-a-bitch! Son-
    Of-a-bitch!' Brahms' 3rd *Symphony*

Is all sex, a blast of brass, a tentative answer,
Then the pounding forth of a tapestry of ecstasy,
    But it's haunted by Schumann's *'Rhenish,'*
    The river not the wine, or maybe both,
        And then Brahms' 3rd evolves
Into misery and hysterical clamor, Schumann
        Without echoes, the student
Reinventing the master, the ruined romantic.
    Johannes Brahms and Clara
    Schumann were off on a concert tour,
Robert at home straining against his bars
        And his strait-jackets: real
        And imaginary, musical and eternal.

EARTH AS A WHEEL

When a star fell I went looking for your lost earring
Like the Sherpa who reached the summit of Everest
A full ten minutes ahead of Sir Edmund Hillary,
    Up there where a nanosecond is a light year.
    But being a nonentity is a lifetime career,
And I preferred your dank lawns and unlit ponds haunted
By ghosts in shining armor and the ambiguous search
    For your vagrant earring—"It's gold!"
    You told me, "With a real diamond!"

I didn't care if it was a shoestring attached to a dead
    Rabbit's foot, the white one we always
    Follow down the tunnel into Wonderland,
Where any time of night or day you can look at the sky
    And see comets, Himalayas, Everest,
Where so many perished and lived forever going up
    And down in sudden whiteouts, chance
Avalanches, collapses and cliffs of sheer exhaustion.
Just as the highest peak on earth is amazing, so is it

    That you are the custodian of this jewel
You keep panicking about, losing and finding, even
    Without my help, so that I must live
    In history with the memory of what
I once achieved, like Tenzing Norgay, that wise Tibetan,
    Smiling up there against dark wind,
Bright sun, face wreathed in fur, glistening, forgotten
    By the world, thinking "Of course it's
    A wheel, but not perceptibly turning."

PERSEPHONE'S CAVE

In winter the sun is nearer the earth than ever,
But what does it matter, every crypto-,
    Proto-lover hidden in holy snow,
    Living only as after-images,
The vivid violet of pigeon feathers
Or cyclamen petals that blossomed
    Under Persephone's heels
As she fled. In February, the toy bear,
The groundhog who lunches on flowerbuds—
Last year the rascal beneath my garage
Ate the tops off all my lilies—comes out to see

How everything is doing. Everything,
    It just so happens, is nothing
    But the puzzle of his shadow.
He peers at this as if to decipher a cause:
"How can I know what it is that I know?"
Then he tries to get back to the solitude
    Of his so-called slumber,
Dreams of brown-eyed woodchuck girls
    And the message he decodes
From the silence at Persephone's cave,
    Which is, *"Wait. Wait for spring*
    Or until it's as warm out there
As it is in here." Or just, *"Wait. Wait."*

The Lunatic from La Mancha

Between myself and death is a windmill
    I must stop with my spear.
Between myself and death is a colander
    I will call a helmet and always wear.
If vigorous hair grows on my tender naked
    Aging skull, perhaps it will poke

Through the holes where water once ran away
    From spaghetti, its Italian ally
And enemy, whose origins were in the Orient,
    But came here on the advice
Of my friend, Sir Marco Polo. May the colander's
    Legs serve my brains as antennae

And frighten my opponents by their resemblance
    To horns. Between myself and death
Is my horse, Rosinante, who provokes laughter
    By the way her spine droops,
Her belly sags, and her eyes widen shyly
    At hints of encouragement. Between myself

And death is the lovely Dulcinea, her sweetness
    Of honey and sunlight on an autumn day.
But winter must come, for even autumn
    Grows bored with my foolishness
And eases away. Between myself and death
    Is the bed on which I'll lie, gaze at the wall,

And whisper, if anyone comes and begs me rise,
    "There are no birds this year
In last year's nests." Therefore no songs in the air,
    Which goes for you too, Sancho Panza:
It isn't nice to criticize a crazy person or make fun.
    Between myself and life is death,

Of course, and the moon that constantly loved me,
    And the earth that so clearly despises us—
"That's not true!" cried Sancho Panza, but the famous
    Lunatic of La Mancha rolled over
To face the wall by his deathbed and murmured,
    "As we have always despised her."

FREE ADVICE

1. To a Worm
    Nothing will work. You are limp
And self-copulating. The closest you come
    To a backbone is the fishhook
That costs you and whoever bites, their life.
    What's the use. You'll drown
In rain anyway, and confuse a weak flashlight
    With the Hercules of day.

2. To Wonder Woman
    All airplanes are transparent.
It's part of the miracle of flight and why
    You've got that ladder and
Lariat for when you feel like going to hell
    And taunting the devil, beautiful
Boots, an ebony peplum, that starry blouse
    And tiara. What do you want?

3. To a Poet
    Comrade Kamikaze, not a minute
Too soon! A loneliness you won't forsake
    Lies at the heart of all your
Preliminaries, and at the heart of loneliness,
    A regret you can't remember
Or name. But your path, ultimately liminal,
    Is perfectly clear: Life is
The same as Death. There's no turning back.

4. To a Professor
Poems and everything else are bad,
Bad! They come from hell like trees. Their beauty
    Lies in their desire to escape, how
They vanish as they reach their truest bloom, as in
    Eurydice to Orpheus, "Adieu!"

5. To God
Relent. Let Christ and everyone else
Climb down from Golgotha, kiss His mother,
    Sister, frustrated lover, Mary,
Elizabeth, and Mary. Everyone else can weep,
    Laugh and kiss. The Jews
Will climb out of the ovens, dance cartwheels.
    The idea of turning water
In wine and wheat into whisky, was a good one.
    We didn't know that reason
Was a lie without the mercy of love or all your
    Miraculous drunken poetry.

6. To Everyone
Trees in fog. Something is
Missing. Is it the boat or the mooring?
    Or merely another inland winter?
It is good to see an unexpected mirror,
    Trees in fog, something missing.

BLACK LAKES

Trapped water, a shimmering mirror of sunset,
    And a forest of bleak, broken trees
    Ruined by rotting roots: a highway
        Or new road blocked the water
    To make a new black lake. In time,
    Their limbs fall off, their trunks break,
    And they stand in the impotent dignity
Of slow decay like Rodin's *Burghers of Calais*.
    They sacrificed themselves

So women and children could stop eating rats
    Or starve to death, or so the British
    Would lift their siege, yet stand,
        According to Auguste Rodin,
    As if they refused to fully grasp
    The cost of this donation, this capital
    Sacrifice or opaque lake, and asked
Each other, without words, even after much recasting,
    To explain, in anguish and bronze.

THE KICK OF A MULE

1.

A muscular mulatto slapped me across the face
For making believe the fat limb of a tree, three
  Lengths of a baseball bat,
  Was a tollgate and I was
Out there governing invisible, imaginary traffic.
He and two friends were racing their bicycles
On the sidewalk which ran around Robin Hood Dell,
  A concert site in Fairmount Park.
  He turned the blind corner
Of the Dell's dull, red, stockade fence,

2.

Hit my stick, and in a rage dismounted his bike,
Walked over and asked me what the fuck
  I was doing. *"Just playing,"*
  I said, and the smooth skin
On his handsome face wrinkled and showed veins
Like those lacing his wrists and biceps, and besides
The smell of blood in my nose when he slapped me,
  Was the sweet, unshakeable scent
  Of his hair pomade, so I coughed
With nausea and his rage turned thoughtfully cold.

3.

"What do you mean, playing, motherfucker?"
He asked and punched me in the ribs so hard
  I couldn't breathe. It was

Like the kick of a mule.
I ran across the park to Ridge Avenue. He and
His friends chased me for the fun of it, though two
Or three times we made hand contact and eye contact,
His black, mine blue. Then they let me
Get away. I hope he's alive in North
Philadelphia or elsewhere, wish we could drink whiskey

4.
Until our minds were the same color and we
Could go back to that minute already
So familiar I'm sure he's forgotten,
So we could revisit and enjoy it, immortal
In amber as a spider or a fly, what Conrad
Described so sweetly in "The Secret Sharer,"
When the uneasy Captain looks down
And observes a naked human swimmer,
And his cigar plops into the clear dark water.

CHAMBER MUSIC

—Mn.

Molly Bloom's first word in *Ulysses*

At dawn the leafless trees arose like smoke.
How patiently the sun awaited for merely gray
To become regal and the court of day,
"All rise!" and so forth, in blue. How clearly
The beginning of the world is the end of the earth,
The sun motionless, our pitiful planet rolling over
In its clouds of balm and its nightmares,
Wondering if it can still snatch another hour,
Another minute, it doesn't matter, of this delicious

Half-oblivion, life's opening to light so awful,
So irresistible. The dog left out all night
Remembers herself and begins to moan.
The canvasser's wife, again alone, her bed linen
Waxy as a candle stowed in the cupboard for when
The power goes out, gets up holding
Her gown round her waist, shuffles to the pot,
Lowers the boom and sits down to pee,
Not a thought in her head that is human.

THE LAST LAMP-LIGHTERS

I saw the last lamp-lighters! Patrolling
    The dusk, looking for gas-lamps
Whose lights had gone out. Each held a pole
Forked for lifting the frail pearl-tinted bowl,
And one with a small wheel and flint for casting

A spark. Did all lamps need to be lit? Or just
    Those doused by raindrops or errant drafts?
They seemed sad, these doomed men who knew
How to give fog its soft perfume, and the facts
Of our life their necessary, tender, but fatal glow.

II.
All That Is Solid Melts into Air
All That Is Solid Melts into Air

We had fed the heart on fantasies,
The heart's grown brutal from the fare;
More substance in our enmities
Than in our love...
—W. B. Yeats, "Meditations in the Time of Civil War"

EMPEDOCLES ON ETNA

The fool ascended until the heat of the cone
    Burned through his shoes and he blamed
His shoes, the rock at the pink lip of the abyss
Polished by novelty, searing the calloused soles
        Of his feet, so he slipped or skipped
        Or leaped recalling in his last blink
    Of consciousness the empty shoes
Standing at the brink, proof of his deranged
    Stupidity, self-hatred so intense he flew
Like a moth, like a wounded goose, into the crater

Of chaos and the inane. Hölderlin said he did it
Because he so loved Mother Earth. (For me
    Read wine, women, and those bubbles
Of jolliness some claim are metaphors of God.)
Others say his brain was unbalanced by his lust
For attention, a craving for fame that mistook
    Lava for poetry, seething with issues
Instead of seizing them as we must, but not
        Empedocles, for whom error
        And Etna were the facts of life.

Do you have trouble thinking logically?
Tend to believe the truth is a paradox
Or inaccessible muddle? Are you unique?
Secretly tired of your words being scattered
Like confetti by the witty but inadequate
    Attention of friends, unknown guests
And free-loaders at your weddings
    Of the soul? Do you lie? Hate
To teach or preach, yet lean that way
Anyhow? Looking for places kindred

    Suckers suffer kindred needs and with
Earnest tenderness pretend to share them?
And would you join a flock of sheep
So wretched they never get fleeced, look like drunks
Who crap in their sleep, huddle and bleat
    As if lost prophets, faces synonymous
With guilt and weak stupidity, for when a wolf
    Rips out the guts of a brother or sister,
Are you mute? Half happily enchanted
By misfortune when it strikes another,

    Uttering 'Bah-ha-ha-ha-ha!' to good
And evil equally? Try poetry. Tell us how life
Is a cruel but precious gift. Join the herd
On the hillside so closely cropped
With envious teeth it can barely grow
    Anything but these weeds purple at twilight

When the moon rises and invisible crickets
    Squeak and twitter, one moon,
One cricket, one poem or lover as good as
A million, and better or worse than another.

CROSSING BROOKLYN FERRY

The sun like a ripe peach
Falls on the spokes of Manhattan and loosens.
It is sunset. The ferry is crossing the river
    That lies east into darkness.
Whitman stands at the back of it, in the stern,
Imagining friendships with the living and dead,
    Gangs of young men and souls
Calling, "Walt! Yo!" offering a casual touch,
The friendly press of a shoulder while walking,
    A knee while sitting, without
Which there's nothing, just this crucifixion of
    Narcissus, his blurred face reflected
    In sunset on the purple water
With shimmering spikes as if Christ's crown
Of thorns, and later His nimbus: *'Goodnight,*
    Beauty. Come again tomorrow
In a glory of pinkness at the absolute crisis
Of solitude so I can bask again awhile in what
    I can feel but never touch, afloat
In a crowd as if not lost, watching the night
Dissolve—how could it all be nothing?—
    Then turning to face you as if
    A street with dark eyes, sunrise!'

BOWL OF CHERRIES

Our sour cherry harvest lay picked
In a glimmering colander two feet wide, one deep,
Stainless steel bright as a mirror. Such luscious
Rudeness, my little wife on her step-stool reaching
    To pluck and receive ambiguous treasures,
    Tooth-breaking if unpitted, from our pitiful
Ever-defended cherry tree, a dwarf over-shadowed
By the grossly enormous maple stolen as a sapling
    From Calvary Cemetery by the old woman
Who came before, the prioress, to replace the elm
    That had died from Dutch fungus disease

And fell against the stable. She must have thought
She'd live forever, marching in her gaunt ageless
    Severity all over our formerly Irish city,
Across the bridge to Calvary in South Portland,
Then back again, the kidnaped orphan hidden
    Beneath her overcoat. It grew like a weed,
My cherry tree fitfully producing its one cheery bowl
Of blood berries, frail bubbles raided by blue jays
    And squirrels, but gratefully consumed
With sugar, the way prospects of a kiss, when life
Gets dull, are improved by cosmetics or a clean shave.

MOMENT OF TRUTH

1.

One must explain a knot is an idea,
A cord applying pressure to itself
Due to a sequence of backward and forward
Loops concluding with the critical insertion
Of loose ends that becomes
An illustration of itself, a flower of no return,
A blossom not easily undone. And sometimes
More cords than one, or crossed boards
Fused for impaling by nailing
Through an enemy's ankles and wrists, the whole
World having a migraine, the sun flashing its light

2.

In lateral lines, the wind dying,
The cypress and sandstone horizon quivering
With the fever that precedes a roar of horror
Or laughter, an acrid human aroma,
Turds and urine stales everywhere, the man
Pausing to murmur in Aramaic, "I can't see
Anymore," and just then a nameless woman—
She has to be nameless, or forget
Her name, Rhonda, Tanya, Jill, or whatever—
Eating her lunch on the street and watching
The disgusting circus pass, hands

3.

Him her purple napkin before wiping yoghurt,
Garlic and hard-boiled egg from her lips, and
    Soon as the man's quicksilver
Divinity imparts its image, she receives, at last,
Her name, Veronica, true likeness, referring
    To her sanitary hanky. In Spain
    A bull about to be killed is offered
The chance to wipe its face in its matador's cape,
The Veronica, which precedes the moment of grace,
    Same uric stench, unintelligible
And kinetic stentor roar and sense of a sun-stunned

4.

    Granite arena, sun-stunted
    Greenery, and the bull lies down
In the heart of the crowd like a child or a woman
About to be named by death and sainted, a flower
Of our entanglement with life not easily undone.
In art there is nothing authentic except the desire
    To impart unto death the human
Likeness, as if to say I'd like to wipe my face in you,
Feet nailed or hanging free of mere gravity, a blossom
    On a rose's stem, the end of a rope,
A transcendence from which there is no return, none.

SIERRA LEONE

In the country called Mountain Lion
People have no hands—tax collectors took them,
And voting regulators, with the swift drop of an ax
    Or machete. Their badges of office
Are the most efficient machine guns on the planet,
Manufactured in Israel and the Czech Republic,
    Their preferred mode of transport

An oyster-white Land Rover with outdoor plumbing
    And cunning winches, from which Sahib,
Pink as a pearl, once shot impala. Remember the poem
Of Robert Frost where the buzz-saw ate the boy's hand
    For supper, called in the American spirit
Of denial, "Out, Out—"? This isn't like that. It's more
The body's dread of becoming a semaphore, and of its fate

As marionette. It's the prophetic wisdom of paranoia
Instructing cruelty and power with blunt precision:
    It's hard to dress and cut bread,
But the heart doesn't fail. The body is a continent,
    And the mind of the world an ill wind
    Whose eyes are bigger than its stomach,
If you'll forgive a minute this pretending to be its parent.

TRIAL BY NATURE

Deep in the ozone of the onion, he was tried
And found guilty: Abuse of the subject. Forty years
    Of obscurity! "But I am the subject..."
He began, and the Blonde Queen gaveled him down:
"Silence in the cunt! Or I'll add ten more for tautology!
    Take him away!" Didn't she mean court?
He wondered, but there was no one to answer.
Bound and shuffling in chains of revisions,
    They led the failed poet into the onion's
    Deepest dungeon, where whiteness hints
Most tenderly at green, and skin is indistinguishable
From hair, imprisoning him far from the crinkle
Of dead paper and the knife preparing to take
    Its tearful slice of reality. He was fed bread,
    Water and mayonnaise until the end
Of his days, with a piece of blue cheese
    Tossed in sometimes on Fridays.

FOUL PLAY

The papers said a man was found dead
Under the George Street Bridge above the Codorus Creek,
No signs of foul play, cause of death unknown, so after
    School, 4th grade, anything better than
Pick-up touch football, other games and friendship crushes
    At which I'd fail, my father and grandmother
Crippled by age and distance, and almost a thousand miles
    Away, I went to explore Lethe's wharf,
Understanding as little about life as the other. I trod
The dull weeds along the filthy Codorus to where some
    Fat ones lay flattened, and sure enough
He was gone. I was whacked by a wave of rancid grease
I instantly recognized as human, ashamed to discover
    What my nose and whole psyche, every
Cell in my gangly frame, already knew about concrete skies,
    Polluted rivers, and a dull, incessant
Overhead roar, so intensely ashamed I didn't brag or tell
Anyone, but prayed to the gods of heaven and hell mindlessly,
    Wordlessly, to live so well by cruelty
And cunning that corruption would be, by the love and pity
Of others, perfumed. And isn't this how we live? And this
    Black flower part of that? No it isn't.
We try to accept and forgive, and not die alone under a bridge.

THE ORIGINS OF TRAGEDY

The harelips, cleft-palates, dwarfs,
    Eyebrows a single weasel
    Stretched across the bone ridge
Of foreheads an inch high brow, the palsied,
Pointy-skulled, clubfooted, grinning,
    Drooling, swallowing, crossing and uncrossing
Their legs and wiggling as if in hopes
    Of easing an itch, yellow-eyed
    As foxes, or pale blue like the sky
Above their homeland, or these two combined
In the same eyes, or alternate in a pair,

Come from their spinach and olive farms,
    Basically smooth-skinned trees
They'd whack on the head anyone who tried
    To cut down for fire, which live
For centuries with little attention or effort,
From flocks of wool, mutton and lamb,
    Recreational sex for the adolescent
And elderly, all self-consciously seat themselves
In a ring of stone benches, where they've seen
    Huge bulls, a half dozen doves, killed

To kindle in them a morsel of religious terror.
Today it's the play by Sophocles, who was a general
    In the army, and a senator. If they
Can catch a glimpse, they see the playwright
    Is tall and undeformed. In his play

A handsome, powerful cripple,
Accidently kills the King his father and marries
    The widow, the Queen his mother,
And gives her four babies. The gap
    In their years could be as small

As fourteen. If Oedipus was twenty when he
Returned to Thebes, Jocasta could be as sweet
    As thirty-four, which is not exactly
    Rotten fish or a dish of leftover eggs
Pulled from the cold cellar where the Greeks
Cured yoghurt and goat cheese. The woman
    Who smelled of cat urine was the beggar
    At the gate with the riddle. To call
Her a sphinx was a gag about her hairiness,
Thankfully invisible, her filth, and of course

Her ripe aroma. There was also a prophet
Whose wisdom comes from a sex-change or two,
    From not being fooled by whatever's
    In front of his sightless eyes, and a gang
Of dancing fools reciting every old hope
And story everyone's known all their lives.
    The country crowd takes home from this,
    Ideas like grains of sand adhere
To a stick to start an island, in this case
    Culture: it's not so good

    To sleep with your sister or mother.
It sows confusion in your kids and shows

The whole world you're isolated and poor.
    Even lame, Oedipus stood a foot or two taller
Than the shepherds and farmers, so he clearly
Was no runt begotten in giggling folly
    By a sister and brother. Clean-featured,
    Six-feet tall meant noble lineage.
He stumbled into an error which was for them
A way of life, a curse and a dirty secret

It was not too late to mend. Who wants to see
Wife and mother hang herself due to a new idea:
    Dishonor? Who wants to squash his eyes
Into blood and wine like grapes? The priest
    Is always right, but knowing the future
    Never saved ought from grief. The chorus,
Like us, is hopeless, but does its best,
And this was made for us by Sophocles,
Who was a soldier, who risked his life so we
    Could be free, not slaves of work or sex.

RIGHT AND WRONG

Wrong is nothing and nowhere and takes
Its name from a great black bottomless lake,
The heart of which pranksters once marked with lipstick
On old newspaper nailed to a cane: "No Swimming,
Hunting or Fishing, Lake Wrong, Ha Ha Ha!"
Right being everything everywhere else. Its lakes
Are teeming with pike, leaping trout
And salmon grimacing as if over-stuffed sandwiches
Yearning for eagles and bears to god dammit
Just take a bite, or meanwhile let's nibble on feathers
And a hook, worms, doughballs, anything.
No invisible cliffs, no slippery slopes, no stairways
Paved with fool's gold, no sliced meat green

As a picnic site beside Lake Right, where everyone's
Greasy with chicken, corn on the cob, swimming
In the refreshing waters of crystalline success,
While all along Lake Wrong they're eating raw crow
And other unmentionables. Nobody says hello, just
"I know, I know." I bought a cottage
On Lake Wrong over fifty years ago.
I was wearing those glasses with the rose quartz
Lenses, rotten-tinted they're called,
Pink and opaque, and for me everything wrong is perfect
As a catbird's infinite, beautiful, meaningless, mocking,
Untranslatable song, which you only hear
Trying to swim Lake Wrong chained to great weights.

PRAYER

Worm says it will swallow no more fishhooks,
Mackerel or trout, red-breasted robin, whatever.
    Mayfly concurs. Fish agrees with fawn,
No more eagles. Termite larvae, the white sleepy kind,
    Blonde or orange-headed, declare
    They've feasted on their last bear,
    Black or grizzly, they're indifferent.
    Mouse renounces cat. Softly whipping
    Its velvet or hairless tail, mouse sees
Eye to eye with starling and sparrow:
'We have to draw the line—*"Chirrup! Squeak!"*—

Somewhere.' Cat says it's Lent as far as
That big dog is concerned, which leaves eagle
And bear gazing at the gold inferno in the sky,
The iron uppermost bough of the hemlock
    Or crag of the gray mountain, silently.
Our ancient terrors all seem to be smiling,
And their smiles are not benign. We won't eat you,
    They seem to be thinking to mountain,
    Tree, and sky, who in turn gaze at space,
Filthy with galaxies and the dry ice of comets.
    And space gazes in prayer at splendor
    Like a black lamb at a flying shadow.

FRANZ SCHUBERT

They put a steel toad in an imaginary garden, but then
    the real one, warts and all,
Hopped along, the jewel in its head inviting one to whack it
    with a stick and get rich quick.
These were the days when genius was a burden like breathing,
    when one could hear its voice
In a piano or violin murmuring, "I too dislike it!" Soon the real
    toad saw the steel one

And was stung to the heart by its shining triumph over feelings,
    by the ease with which it reflected
Infinite, impervious replication, the apocalypse of life and art.
    The real toad began its *Winterreise,*
Which concluded eventually on a hillside orchard beneath
    a sky with three suns,
As if the madness of a toad could become as potent as song,
    which encouraged it to keep going

Or trying, again and again, as if always getting it wrong.
    Schubert's greatest symphony
Was unfinished when he died of a poison contracted during
    a interchangeable,
Immemorial excitement. "Franz," friends would ask him,
    winking at each other,
"How do you write so many tunes?" And he'd reply, "When
    I finish one, then I begin another. Why?"

THE COLD THAT OWNS US

Why so sore, throat? I did nothing bad to you:
    No kisses or cigars, no second hand smoke.
Do I detect an up-and-coming disgrace
    With fate? Why is life such a rough
Patch of over-excited chemicals in a bag of skin
    So beautiful and yet so barely adequate

Every piece of the puzzle, ankles, knees, throat,
    Not to mention the heart or core, sooner
Or later, in surrender or revolt? In the end we return
    To the stars that made us, and to the cold
That owns us, and irresistibly fall like motes
    From fortune and men's eyes.

III.
Maps of Clamor
Maps of Clamor

Noisemakers shoot into the light: it's the Truth
breaking the news.

—Paul Celan

FIREWOOD

How do you cut down a tree in Bulgaria?
    A little at a time, if illegal,
    A chip as if to mark a path, another
On a day later as if you suddenly needed
    To pick your teeth or fashion
A home-made match and just happened
    To get caught short with your ax.
    In a year, the tree won't know
What hit it. It'll lie down like I did
    At the foot of an iron stairway,

My waterbottle of home-made wine
    Blurting from under my elbow
    Like a red football fumbled forever,
And not before banging the hell
Out of my ribs. The wine vanished
    Like sap from a tree, leaving only
    Dampness and a sentimental smell—
I could have loved you, I reasoned,
Assessing the blush of its bouquet.
    If you lack a Balkan ax, all iron face,

But otherwise nearly pin-headed,
Or public stairs with broken iron treads
    Such as *Makedonski Ploshtád*,
Lean on a tree until it gets discouraged
    And falls down, or forage
    Like the ancient babushka

In black skirt and black sweater
Who couldn't climb over the bank
    Of the *Bistriça,* it got so cold
The moment the sun drooped below
The mountain bowl. She wouldn't

Let go of a branch somebody lost
Or tossed away. I'd been jogging
    By the river. "Thank you,
Stupid *Amerikanetz,*" she whispered as I helped
Her and her firewood over the bank. *"Molyah,"*
    She said. Trees are like people,
Whatever you can get home and keep
    Is good wood. I wasn't taking
    Her anywhere, but she looked
    Me over as if she wasn't sure.

BALKANS ON THE BRAIN

1.

Vision is an act of imagining, hence susceptible
To poison, dreams and drugs. It is *re*-cognition,

As whenever first doused you told yourself,
"Again!" How could this both be and have been?

Gradually blind spots and smears get replaced
By an aurora borealis of anguish, a Balkan necktie

Collection of ochre, cobalt, zeroes and worms,
Dating from the days of God's child's play.

2.

Rocks lodge like *Stara Planina* in the brain's
Crenelations, shards of Lucifer, spikes of Christ,

And the light from Faust's borrowed mirror,
Another pact obscured by clarity and the fact

That it's still there, we're still here, with an
Emotional overload and back-up—one blood vessel

Shrinking or swelling, rattling the optic nerve's
Necessarily loose connection, understanding's

3.

Necessarily loose connection, for how could
Understanding be otherwise? One fatal

Cherveyno vino, organ meat or crustacean indulgence,
Sausage or bowl of *bop chorbá,* could add

To the blood that final crystal of uric acid
Which precipitates an event so piercing

All previous headaches seem like baby-thought—
That redhead in boots, those Balkans on the brain.

REASONS FOR MLADIC'S
BEHAVIOR AT SREBRENICA

The road of life is long and hard. Guidance
Is rare as a goose, even when the goose is well-cooked.
    The Dutch colonel in charge of those chicken-shit
U.N. troops had a Turkish moustache. Five hundred years
    Of the yoke, why forget? The hotel was full
And there wasn't a cab. Say whatever comes into mind
If it's all you've got in your head. Those Bosnian Muslims
Were sons-of-bitches, deadly Goliaths right from the Bible.
    War is hell, and sometimes a massacre or two
Makes you sure you're in it, Mladic no more a medieval

Troglodyte fit to fight with club and spear than over half
    The world: one generation without the history
Of poetry and anyone's a village bully. Suddenly there's
State-of-the-art pushbutton weaponry up the yin-yang.
    Under Communism, even Tito, you tended
    To be bullied by experts: pulling the trigger
On Czech automatics sets you free. Those Muslim refugees
Looked wretched, interfering with our goals of a superior
    Hollywood in Yugoslavia. Therefore slaughter them
All in schoolrooms, warehouses, forests and fields,

And bulldoze their bodies into pits of Balkan fertility.
You can get rid of 8,000 in four or five days, less than it takes
For a letter to arrive from Belgrade, let alone a medal.
    Evil is tone-deaf and vice versa. Mladic enjoyed
Making the mothers smile by giving candybars to their kids

And promising transport for the elderly, but sooner or later
    He had to get down to business in order
To have a good night's rest. Yet there's always a problem:
    How do you wipe your boots if your room
Has no curtains? Evil is tone-deaf. I meant that about poetry.

BALKAN BOY

"If you see one, beat him. He will know what he's done."

—Bulgarian proverb

To behave like a man, a boy demands
    Of his mother, *"Zashtó me*
Tziganish pred vsíchki?" his face suddenly
    Dark as a tree: "Why do you
Make me a gypsy in front of the others?"
The mother blubbering and bullying
Before saying goodby for awhile, so after
A half hour, or just fifteen minutes,
    The boy, as if entering
    The army, calmed down

    And took pity on worry,
Kisses and tears. You too are a gypsy,
    And would make me one
    If I were so lucky. Why
Do you slip me into your purse, condemned
To the secrecy of darkness and lint? Why
Do you treat me like a yo-yo? Throw me
    A purple scarf and a gold chain.
Calm down for awhile and take pity
    So I can pretend to have dignity.

BALKAN MOSQUITO

Pancreationism meant henceforward lions would mate
    with lambs,
And even worms copulate with slithering fishes. The parrot
    could now flap its wings
Above an obediently squatting chimpanzee. But in Belgrade
    things went wrong:

There a mosquito humping an elephant discovered that his
    paramour had perished
From a heart-attack: orgasm among pachyderms packs
    a terrible cardiac wallop."O my Christ!"
Whined the mosquito, reaching for his shovel, "a moment
    of pleasure, then a lifetime of digging."

Let us remember the laboring mosquito when we toast the
    success in Serbia
Of Vojislav Kostunica, and give earth a little wine for a largeness
    of heart that no longer pumps blood.
The elephant was not named Milosevic, who's he? It was named
    Yugoslavia.

BITES FROM THE STAFF OF LIFE

The men sat around a long table lit with wine
And a candelabra. Each held their own loaf
Of bread from which they stole a few bites
    And chewed, but waited for the priest
Before starting their wine. Slices of lemon floated
In everyone's water-glass like sections of the moon,
Like wheels torn from a child's toy wagon. Women
    Theatrically bored, but inclined to mischief,
Sat as if inhibited by national ideas of modesty,
    Blondes with ebony ditches in their hair,
    Or straightforward unfolded crows' wings,
    Breasts like puppies nosing toward heaven,
Aunts and grandmothers who'd tinted chin whiskers
    With peroxide, but who cares? Love
    Is the art of the possible—uncertainty,

Whether hopeless or charming, is eventually fatal.
    "Drink while your glass is full!"
Cried the priest, lifting his foot-high silver cross
    In its bouquet of soaked geraniums,
Touching it one at a time to each brow. "It'll someday
Be empty! Kiss while your lips are young, so that when
    You are old you'll remember that once
Your lips have been kissed!" The prettier women made
    Faces at God as the men all solemnly
    Drank to this, everyone's eyes darkly shining,
The wine, the room, our heads dripping with water

Made holy by the health of geraniums and of prayer,
Except for the bread from which the men had taken
    Those early white bites before the blessing,
      Cheating of course, but that's life.

DEMOLISHING THE TOMB

They blew up Dimitrov's mausoleum,
Tomb of the only mummy still in Europe outside
    Of Moscow, though maybe Hoxha
In Albania, or even Tito, we don't know. It fell
    To dynamite on a Monday
Because they didn't use sufficient explosives
The previous Sunday, crypt a dozen stories deep,

Lined with lead and concrete, braced by iron.
    Gypsy beggars who claimed the park
Of the tomb as turf, felt unsafe, were not amused
    By this outburst of national exuberance:
    "There'll be a Nuremberg Trial!" cried
    A fat woman, smiling but striving
To act earnest. "They should shoot the president!"

Grinned a toothless fellow, taunting her: Stoyanov
    A new blue, though some say an old red.
"They wanted to bury the whole Central Committee
    In there," chimed in another patriot
Who didn't care if he knew exactly what he said:
"They shouldn't have turned the center of Sofia
    Into a cemetery!" Is this obvious?

On the steps of the Sheraton, a hard-working
    Businessman was complaining,
"Ot pradnyá boyá né se právy!" ("You can't
    Make paint from a fart!") though

Not referring to dismantling for public show
　　And Euro-community hopes the tomb
Of the parent of Bulgarian communism, party

　　Of bitter rationalists, and the honest
But unlucky, Giorgy Dimitrov, creator of World War
　　II's "Popular Front" and a plan
With Tito to yoke Bulgaria with Yugoslavia,
　　Provoking Stalin's anger and eventual
Intervention: Dimitrov's last days in that Soviet
　　Health Sanitorium were a little touch

　　And mostly go. With poisoned food,
You're dead if you do, but dead if you don't.
Dimitrov's tomb was apparently an air-raid shelter.
　　But when shame takes revenge on history,
　　It loves to obliterate understanding,
　　To stoke and comfort stupidity. Blame
Is the essence of politics, of provisional fixing.

GADJO DJILO

A girl scowls, a true *farouche*, a rose
With thorns for eyebrows. A boy is lost
    Among strangers. The girl declines
To translate for the boy, his *French* too akin
    To her ex-husband's. Girl displays
Contempt by mooning boy. Smooth moons,
    Tender thorns. Girl gathers stove
Wood, bent over like a crone. Bundle snags
    On limb. Boy seeks to untangle
Brush and tree. Girl bites boy's naked wrist.

    Boy says "Ow!" but smiles kindly.
Girl stomps away, but now appears curious.
    Soon the acquaintance accelerates:
Collisions, apologies, winks and grin. If W
    Is here, can X be far behind?
Remember to be helpful to girls who scowl.
    Nod politely when they bite you,
But it's also important to acknowledge a girl's
    True power and say "Ow!" You're
Almost in the clear. Look up the word *farouche*.

METAL PICKERS

Two pretty gypsies, diseased thieves
In the local perspective, entered the yard
Where a Bulgarian car mechanic rebuilt wrecks
He hammered and welded together
From spare engines and car bodies,
No helmet or goggles: safety last.
Beside his fence, plum trees and daffodils
And grape vines raised black arms
For enough warmth to untwist green tendrils
And pink leaves. The mechanic's sons or apprentices
Watched the women approach in shocked paralysis:
They were begging for metal, their ancestors
From lower Asia being smelters, and whoever disposed
Of nightsoil and dead men. The welder turned off
The lilac tip of his torch and bestowed on them
Unimaginable treasure, fenders, manifolds and bumpers
The ladies hauled away without wasting a scrap.
They wore wool leggings embroidered in figures
Retelling their stories of family and race,
Chains of wanderings, sorrow, joy and speculation
Wherein everyone's a prisoner awhile,
Bulgarian or Roma. One wore her ponytail
In a rubber band, her girlfriend, with whom
She consulted in fierce whispers,
A plated gold barrette she obviously
Passionately intended to save. (*"You're so stupid!"*
She told me later. "You want my barrette?
You can have it for nothing. Here!")

THE BRIDGE AT MITROVICA

"It happened. So what?"
      —General Klaus Reinhardt,
           on the theft of his personal revolver during a
           demonstration of pro-NATO feelings.
           (*New York Times,* Feb. 28, 2000)

The Ibar runs through Mitroviça,
Fast as a mermaid and filled with black truth,
Or trout—but so what, running under the bridge
      Where General Klaus Reinhardt
Described sense and moderation—'*Make love*
      To your neighbor, not war!'—
To a whirlpool of twenty-five thousand earnest,
Deserving Albanians, incensed by the persistence
      Of three thousand Serbian obstacles
To total possession of the city's north side—

Red flags, black eagles rampant. But during
      The swim of confusion, so many hands
Eager to touch and bless for luck their KFOR
      Benefactor, someone unhooked
And whisked from the general's holster his pistol,
Which unlike the local Serbian remnant, is safe
      In the belly of a fairytale fish. So what?
O Ibar, black Ibar, river of life, tell me why
Must you run so fast? I wait for the moon
      All day, for the sun all night. ·

IV.
A Portion for Foxes

A Portion for Foxes

But those that seek my soul to destroy it, shall
go into the lower parts of the earth.
They shall fall by the sword: they shall be a
portion for foxes.

—Psalm 63

CHAIRMAN MAO SWIMMING

It was a hot summer of course. Human turds
Floated in the Pearl River below Guangzhou.
Chairman Mao directed his sailing yacht
    Into the middle of it, climbed down
A rope ladder, splashed and drifted on his back
    A half dozen miles in white boxer
Shorts, leather sandals still aboard ship,
Belly like a tan dirigible, a dome:

"Why are you so afraid of dirt?" he teased
His bodyguards and doctors. "Could a fish
    Survive in distilled water?"
It's a peasant story, the way Khrushchev
Mispronounced *fat* at the Kennedys' table:
    "*Faht,*" he said, declining
Their lobster thermidor, "Oh no, I'm afraid
    It make me *faht!*" Discerning

    His error in Jackie Kennedy's
Paralysis of horror, he aggravated matters
    Further with his apology, blub-blub-blub
    Noises from his lips to imitate
    Escaping gas, then pretending
To heave his stomach with both hands
To explain the difference between words
He pronounced identically: *faht* and *faht*.

Thus farmers govern animals by knowledge
Of their weaknesses: addiction to food,

Fear of stick or wolf, tenderness
In the bull's nose where he wears his ring,
    Fever of roosters for hens, or why
    The males' wings needn't be clipped,
    Even the love of a boar for mud ripe

With its own manure, along with a pail or two
Of swill which keeps it from tearing through
    Flimsy barbed wire. Mao
Was lured from the furious whirlpools
Of the Yangtze in his homeland Hunan
    By promises of lunch: "Okay," he said,
After two hours of the dead-man's float,

    "Let's eat." He skipped the Yellow
    Because of silt, and after the filth
Of the Pearl, swam in the northern rivers,
The Xiang and the dangerous Yangtze,
Where he resolved to build a dam and transform
The Three Gorges, revered by poets and painters
    For centuries, into a huge reservoir,
Because for a peasant life is a struggle

Against power and the management of horror.
    Mao wrote,
        "We will make a stone wall against
    the upper river to the west and hold back
    steamy clouds and rain of Wu peaks. Over tall chasms
        will be a calm lake, and if the goddess
    of these mountains is not dead, she will marvel
    at the changed world!"
                And he called it a poem.

AFRICA

The children, teenagers, very black, stood five feet tall,
    and paid for their spilled
Cornucopia of American food with a hundred dollars in
    food stamps,
But it wasn't enough, so one ran off to the parking lot,
    nearly twin to the goose
Who absent-mindedly balanced a peanut-butter jar
    on her head,

And came back with a ten-dollar bill to flick at the other's
    glances
With the African equivalent of a Gallic shrug, *'This is a truth*
    I accept
But do not love!' and passed it to the red-haired, patient,
    American cashier.
They spoke in bird cries, fidgeting as if needing to go
    somewhere, but explained

In polite English they came from Zaire. Then they were gone,
    who stood as tall
As those poles topped with skulls adorning the porch of
    Konrad Korzeniowski's
Kurtz before his fevers of murderous eminence turned him
    into a totem
Muttering. Zaire was the Congo, and is now the Congo again.
    I studied their elegant departure

The way Marlow gazed at the snake at the heart of a Belgian
    map: Africa, river,
Polish canary in English drag wanting to be swallowed
    as if complete submission
Was the secret whereby he'd resist becoming a power
    on the earth.
But how could these lovely, ebony teenagers swallow me?

SINAI

Was it right or wrong to adore fire, or evil to worship gold,
    flee murder and slavery,
To cast bricks out of nothing, drive eunuch mules and family
    through sand endlessly,
To say a light in the bush uttered commands? Not even sand
    lasts forever, nor love or an era.

Above was the ignorant sun, the one that stood still for Joshua
    as if to listen, as if its mystery
Were a gift and prayer was a joke, a roar of shouts, a blur of
    trumpets, as the wall like a
Volcano falling, rose up and split. What was dangerous as
    red jelly is safe, black as glass,

Susceptible to polishing if you have all day and night, earth
    a goat, the volcano its cloven hoof,
Earth a pig, the wall its foolish trotter. Bow down. Eat of its
    meat, which is dirt
Or whatever grows from it. Or else don't live, wander
    with your sacks of unleavened bread,

Which is life without law, a stone without the claw of fire
    to engrave its message: bow down,
Accept on your back and neck the touch of God—*THIS IS
    WHO YOU ARE!*—
Seek mercy, praise year after year, minute after minute,
    everything, even the ashes and scars.

BLUEBEARD'S WAY

1. The Castle

People of livid distinction live here, whose speech
Surmounts clenched teeth as if abrupt surf
    Were punishing hidden cliffs: French.
And this is his house, as when a nerve is naked to air
    Is called *frank*, or a wound
To skin or bone, an *insult*.
Love's memory? It's like fresh meat: if not
Kept cold, it rots and crawls. Such things
As history are perfected by truth and realism,
So every wall of Bluebeard's mausoleum
    Was lined by trunks of human oak, as if
    Nakedness were a principle of language
Which after love and caresses should be preserved
For the pleasure of vocabulary refreshed by just
    Such evidence of difference and definition.
Wives and lovers are never victims of people like him,
But of their own susceptibility to personal drama,
    And alert but deceptive antennae.

2. Favorite Opera

'*Love's essence is transience...*' goes the overture,
    And the illusion of cathexis
Is the reflex of a calf bleating, or else a cow's vanity:
    Donna Anna, sampled then abandoned, ruining
The tune with her sightings and ambulance alarms:

"Don Gio-VANNI!" She believes God is a tenor
And Satan a baritone. Bluebeard agrees.
He thinks God is an angel, boy or girl, that nothing
 Is forever, love is the test of something,
 Or a rehearsal, and all of life a tease.

3. Reasons Are Not Motives
 It is bitter how things come and go,
 And neither for worse nor for better.
 A spouse should be dressed in white
With veils like candlelight in a lantern, like a worm
 In a tented web, doomed to turn
 Into a moth doomed to burn
 Someone with its saliva. See how
 An appetite floods the beach,
Slaps the seawall with bleachwater and alabaster,
Then eases away leaving behind the bride,
 That accident of yesterday.

4. The Key
One hand washes another, but as one becomes pure,
 The other gets filthy. A paradox is not a mystery.
The key to the room where the bodies were hung
 Was red and blue forever. Look at the street
After a rain. Only a dead worm never turns.
 In matters of reality, nobody's hands are clean.
The girl in love with her father or the boy who pursues a fool
 Finds Bluebeard's castle. But even a lock
Can be taught to forget a key. A paradox is not a mystery.

5. Constructions of Gender

Face and ponytail parody the horse and whip:
Her refusals of curls, chignons, bangs or valence
    To shield her vault of thought, peer
Out from under as if to whisper, "I haven't a clue,
You big strong Bluebeard you!" Tie-dyed crewcuts,
    Tattoos, body piercings, studs and coils
    In navel and nose, shavings, growths
And slouches: all of them emblems of slavery
    To a girlish and maternal wish

    To shelter life from death's withholdings,
And still declare herself inadequate to this. A rabbit
    At the bottom of the pit that traps a tiger and
Whimpers: "We're both in this together!"
Isn't it strange to. disallow our other, truly
    Tenderer desires as ignoble and queer?
    It's like Bluebeard being questioned
On charges of kidnap, rape and murder: puzzled,
    He explains, "I did it for pleasure."

BENJAMIN'S METAPHOR

High in the Pyrenees, at a border that clarifies the difference
    between French granite and Spanish cypress,
Expecting torment if not torture at this sunny and sundry
    acme of human intelligence,

Life's exertion became a tautology, and the proud, otherwise
    shy, unprepossessing Jew
With a scant moustache and round eyeglasses, swallowed
    his lot and ended it,

The lucent, unexpected mind of Walter Benjamin, self-
    obliterated (cyanide
In a vest pocket). The obvious is hard to articulate. He
    proposed the origin of art

In the difficulty of what someone thinks, produced by
    an individual *"No longer able*
To express himself by giving examples of his most important
    concerns." So if you'd hope

To utter more than lullabies or prayers at mealtime, go to
    the Pyrenees of your life,
Where nothing makes sense, and invent the necessity of death
    word for unnecessary word.

ARIADNE'S WEB

Eagerly pacing the labyrinth,
A thread like a wedding band tied to his thick pinky,
His naked blade drooling like a tooth, Theseus,
    The meathead of Athens, is actually
    Standing still: it is only the betrayed,
Drinking and thinking, abandoned to the fogs
Of Naxos by her brother's brainless killer
So he'd be free to pursue Phaedre, her reluctant,

Younger, and prettier sister, giving herself therefore
To the worship of Bacchus—it is Ariadne, smelling
    Of wine and saltwater, knelt at the edge
Of horror, who is truly moving. So hold still,
Little spider. Sip some of this. Close your eyes
    And bite me with the teeth of the mouth
    Of your belly. Tie me up in the almost
Invisible silk of your skin to save for a morsel later.

Il Piombo

Hemingway uttered the mystery: a story
    Is as strong as what it deliberately omits—
And this must be its most important thing, its key.
As in, "I'm in trouble at home," she says, then he:
"What did he say?" And she, "That's between
    Him and me!" In Hemingway's fishing-
In-Switzerland story, the young American brings
Along beautiful bamboo rods, but no *piombo*,
    No pinch of lead; his catgut leaders
Will float on the rigid sapphire Alpine waters,
    Plump trout, orange and blue as sunset, all
    Slumbering out of harm's way, waiting
For crippled locusts to fall from the sky, or a worm

To dance the twist where it hurts, saying *"Ouch, ouch!"*
    If worms uttered words. Many years later,
    Hemingway revealed how Peduzzi had died,
The little Swiss drunkard who'd led the sulky wife
    And fat American along the illegal river,
    Whining in dialect Italian and Tyrolean
To borrow four lire he'd squander on grappa, marc,
    Or rakia, to free his mind from gravity,
    Which makes no sense: sense is grave,
Or the way he hung himself by the neck until dead—
    He had promised to buy salami and bread,
Minnows and lead—*piombo*, according to Hemingway,
    To give the string of a story its weight.

POGIES

Pogies, or menhaden, beloved by bluefish
And my grandfather, have flesh like cornmeal
Boiled until white mush. Russian factory ships,
        Back when we still thought Communism
Could bury us, used to hover along the Maine coast,
Hoovering up millions of the stupid pouting staring
        Silver little idiots for conversion into

        Agricultural fertilizer. Of course
Everything gets converted into fertilizer, but this
Was, by Soviet standards, scientific. My grandfather
        Would rest his false teeth, a full set
        Of double choppers, on a dry saucer,
Neatly gumming their meat from their bones until
He had a stack of heads, spines and tails as tall

        As a napkin rack. He ate with a kind
Of happy gloom, as if in pogies was the essence
        Of mindlessness required for sex and death,
        For the fever of life to achieve its appropriate
Suicidal pitch, the way pogies will beach themselves
        En masse, impelled by terror and self-disgust.
My grandmother sheltered her enormous bunions

In his worn-out, cast-off shoes from which she'd
        Torn away the tongues, discarded
The laces, shuffling back and forth to the alcove
With the kitchen stove bearing more boiled pogies,

While my grandfather gazed into space
And sang some wordless nonsense, *Di di dee di di di,*
From the Russian Ukraine where he was born, running

From home at ten or eleven. When he died
He lied to the nurse from a Boston hospital
About his age in the spirit of a pogie seeking to mate
And escape, even if it killed him. His sons all
Tried to emulate, transcend or understand him,
Or to possess the jewel he'd swallowed
Somewhere along the line, from the belly of a fish.

ADVICE FOR PEDESTRIANS

The best way to deal with a beggar
Who gets in your face in the street,
Is to seize his crutch and beat him on the head
With it until he lies on the sidewalk spitting blood.
It's obvious he wants more than your money.
He wants your house, your car, your children,
Your wife, your job. Teach him

How you're young and lucky, whole in the limbs,
And have always resisted temptation.
"There was a ship," he begins.
Or there was country, there was a war. Militias
Came, then airplanes representing the will
Of the international community.
There's always something. Why not a woman,

A hill at the edge of the city, a capricious
And complicitous moon, a bag
With a bottle of practical coffee brandy? Now's
When you grab that crutch and whack him until
He thinks twice about trying to live
In the wrong place at the wrong time with women,
Bottles, the rich, powerful, vindictive, elusive moon.

MISTLETOE COUNTRY

Hedy Lamarr passed away, Delilah to our Samson,
The velvet-lipped and lidded Victor Mature,
    Who'd rested his donkey-long head
In the Indian sub-continent of Hedy's spice country,
    And paid with his raven locks and his eyes.
    How Hedy quivered with love and remorse,
    A genuine Helen for America's Philistia,
    Who'd earlier floated in *Ecstasy*

To display her ebony arrowhead on the silver screen,
A Hollywood first. They say she invented "Spread
    Spectrum Technology," crucial
To modern microchips and the World Wide Web.
    A related variant, "Frequency Hopping,"
    Played a role in the Bay of Pigs Invasion,
    For which Hedy received nary a penny:
        "I guess they take the idea

And just forget the people," she liked to explain.
Love lies, life tells the truth: Samson was shorn,
    Delilah fleeced, and the world stands
Wide-eyed and forlorn. In L.A. look for a mistletoe
    High in the branches of a naked oak
    Or eucalyptus, and bite your tongue
        For Hedy LaMarr, harder
    As if you deserve the taste of her kiss.

V.
A Spy Among Bacchae
A Spy Among Bacchae

—it's not as if
God fills the waters with mad spawning shapes
or loads the vine with grapes, the palm with dates,
or makes the bull dilate to take the peach
or the plum tremble at the ox's reek,
or the sun cover the pale moon.
                    —D. M. Thomas, *The White Hotel*

LOCOMOTIVE

Let the heart keep beating like a train: *Women, women,*
    women, women...
Let it pretend to discover the meaning of night with its
    puny light gleaming on the rails
Of its simple freedom, its so-called 'headlight' set bluntly
    in the middle of its moon

Of a face like a nose: *Women, women, women, women...*
Trees, darkness, a midnight lamp, a sleeping city, an empty
    station. Suddenly another train
Comes passing the opposite way. It's too fast to see, but one train
    suffers the need

To utter its wail to the other: *"The heart is a train... ah*
    Woo-oh wooh!"
Women, women, women, women... Sometimes the way the train
    slows down
Is quite repulsive. Hunger entangled with hope, both unrequited:
    Maybe, maybe, maybe, maybe.

More, more, more, more. Kiss me, kiss me, kiss me, kiss me.
If sex is oppressive and so often considered evil, it's because
    it is motherly.
Yes, of course it is motherly. It knows what's good for us. You just
    wait. You've had enough.

Mother is busy. Yet sometimes all at once the stars rise with
    the moon

Above a lake that makes everything clear, a mirror of water,
   but what is it?
All you can know is silver tarnished by darkness, the glitter of
   Night, the mother and sex.

(for Boris Hristos, somewhere in the Rhodope Mts.)

BREAKFAST IN VALHALLA

Breakfast of champions was pink bacon,
British style, as if sliced from the living pig
    And seared in the pan, served as a rasher
    On a little personal platter, wet as worms
And still capable of crawling, none of your bogus
Hocus pocus soybean meat-substitute ironed flat
    And decorous as a striped shirt collar.
The heroes gathered in an age- and soot-blackened
Lodge beside Moosehead Lake. Our breakfast

    Servers were old lovers whose names
And faces we could not quite remember, and their
Homelier, resentful, still interfering sisters. Trying
To place them made us tenderly smile: "I know
You got on top of me in the car, but I can't..."
    It was a blonde from Chebeague who knew
What she wanted, at least for ten minutes, then
Married her boyfriend anyway. Look
At these hags, these prunes, everything sunk

From their breasts to their bottoms and turning purple,
    Hair suitable for polishing pots, as if
The joke patch where the Tigris and Euphrates
Converged had asserted itself on top as a last laugh,
    Replacing the silken banners of heavier
    Gold, chestnut and mahogany, iron-ore
Rose or crow's-wing onyx that once flattered
    Our knightly tournaments of jousting
By fluttering. Enough of that. We were waiting

For pancakes soaked in syrup and butter,
Not wanting to eat our bacon too fast, ourselves
Hairless as pigs who gobbled, grunted, stared,
    A life of appetite and anger whittled
To this unintelligible, corpulent point: mirthless
Stupidity, and an old woman's question, pungent
As smoke from the kitchen, that hung in the air:
"Was this *the meaning of life?"* But we couldn't
    Understand what she meant, nor answer.

CITY OF BROTHERLY LOVE

In the bushes outside the art museum,
Where I thought I'd hide my foolishly huge bicycle,
A birthday gift from my adoring *Bobbi*, some boys
    From Brewerytown beyond the Parkway
Had surrounded a pair of girls and were copping feels
Like wolves isolating a lamb and ewe, yipping, nipping,
    Reddening their fleece, while the herd
Of art lovers grazed complacently, lids half-lowered, lips
    Half-raised, nibbling fingertips in worry
For St. Sebastian, so beautiful and dart pierced,
    One after another within their Parthenon

Of yellow bricks, in love with the murmur
Of the mute and immemorial. The girls, one older, one
Younger, were also mute, wordlessly slapping the boys'
Paws away, glancing at each other, while their happy
    Marauders assessed their bodies for fresh targets,
Dodging scratches and grabbing, and I, eleven or twelve,
A still unravished bride astride my mastadon Schwinn
    Phantom, pondered this wild pursuit,
These maidens loath, mind boggled by silent melodies,
Sweet pipes and grainy tambourines, the frenzy of lust
Plucking at the branches of the girls' tender splendor.

At someone's whistle the boys dispersed, dashing across
The lawn of trees and grass to the Schuylkill River Basin,
    And the girls blushed, tidied their skirts
And blouses with girlish grief of fatalism and helpless

Stupefaction, beauty is truth and so forth,
The museum an urn of canvases and pigments, ideas
And ashes, while in its sylvan fringes flourished sex
    And slaughter, as if life were the stones
Stained with life, white sun, blue sky, the march of waves
    Across the wine-red Aegean and Adriatic
Composing a key to an endless, richly true, savage dawn.

UNCLE RUBY

I saw uncle Ruby once in my life—at my aunt Anne's
Fortieth birthday—making jokes about his recent
    Vasectomy, waving a flat be-ringed hand
    Below his waist: "Just a toy," he explained,
    With alien mirth and cunning, as if a Russian
Or Ukrainian Jew, instead of a more cultured German
    Or western type, my mother's sisters'
And their brother's *preferred*, not a mere mysterious
Litvak fraud. Ruby had come with my grandfather's
    Second marriage, so he was half-brother to Anne,
    But only step-brother to my mother, her sisters,
And their brother Philip, who like me took after
    The venerated patriarch, Jacob or Stephen,
We're not sure—Selig Zamachansky, is one rumor:
    Rabinowitz the name on papers purchased

    From some long forgotten eponymous Jake,
    To avoid the army, immigrate, escape—
A blue-eyed overweight maniac addicted to silence,
Noise, and a delirium of superiority, so naturally
Quite vulnerable and requiring the consolations
    Of over-sexed women. When Ruby's mother
    Died of cancer, my grandfather ran away
With wife three. In Montclair we grinned at Ruby's
    Clownish gesture, his hand suggesting
    The knife that cut the cord, fanning
What was too hot to touch in public, myself,

My other uncle, cousins, parents, aunts,
That grandfather already lost in the stratosphere of wife
Four or five—Jake, my mother called
This Esau, a bull outsmarting his brother of his pottage.

ROMAN PEDAGOGY

Roman children prancing in pastures of wildflowers
    and grass, would pause
To stroke the unsloped walls of polished obelisks,
    immense erections
Of white and black granite—there was an illustrious
    rose one somewhere,
Pink quartz. The kids would shudder and suffer
    a terrifying thrill.
Herms, they were called, after the Greek god of
    quicksilver truths,
And were installed all over the semi-domestic
    wilderness by priests
On the orders of senators absorbed in such issues
    of empire as enslavement,

Looting, war. But to protect their children from foolish
    pleasure,
These immense phalloi were lifted into the breeze
    and sun, and at their touch,
Underage Romans remembered to remain in the precincts
    of chastity, docile as heifers
And young bulls grazing beside electric fencing, the shock
    of the rock wholly salutary,
If neither descriptive nor realistic, like metaphor in poetry,
    which is tutelary,
Only ideally instructive, pulling you into a fissure in reality,
    into the startling,
Where it fences and seduces you, changes you like sex
    into what you always were before.

Among School Children

Breasts like unbaked loaves with unimaginable
Nipples, as clad in athletic bras—her parents
    Send her to St. Michael's during the year,
So no doubt keep an eye on her ornaments—
    Only twenty, if not nineteen, blonde
And fully conscious of her potential palette,
    Hence sprawling in this introduction
To literature summer class in pink seersucker

Shorts so loose you could peer up her suntanned
    Thighs into shadowland, a black
Chemise lined with black lace as if underwear,
Held in place by thin black straps against her
    Soft bronze shoulders—stupid,
Brooding, blue-eyed, but not exactly beautiful:
    A rabbit-like overbite gave
    Her upper lip that vague hair-

Fretted look of nervous Swedes and Irishwomen.
But how does one get past the thin amiable spin
    Of her chatter? Or her aroma
Of a rubbery bathtub toy? God as a swan the size
Of a powerboat could dive-bomb her from heaven
    To shoot a cloud up her legs,
Or else conjure her into cowhood and chase her
To Asia, wild-eyed, hoofs flying, squealing

In a corner as he forced his business
Up her Bosporus, so she could sense,
If not understand, sex was vicious, degrading,
Better to use her brain and stop tempting the gods,
Who wasted such luscious endowments
On a teenager. Driving home from school, humidity
Was so dense the sky sprinkled my windshield
With a few drops without ever beginning to rain.

TABULA RASA

Alzheimer's is nature's way of telling us
It doesn't matter. So is death. But getting tired
Of one's concerns is not like losing them totally
    And forever. Nature's way is so many
Broken and fallen trees, no one can walk or see.
    Let's get out of the woods and take
A nap in the park awhile. We'll need a checkered
Tablecloth, a basket of fried chicken, hot or cold,
    We can wash down with Beaujolais

    Until twilight falls and we can't feel,
Let alone notice, the crumbs on our fingers and
Cheeks, only taste salt and delicious grease.
    When the moon comes up we'll be
In a heaven of awe and as silent as she is, but
Only if you can forgive my awkwardness,
    Forgetfulness and demented stupidity,
As I must forgive your intoxicating and sometimes
Over-adventurous naked and impeccable *tabula rasa.*

JEWISH ARTIST

Three naked women float in the air above a cherry orchard
    in full bloom, and don't apologize.
They are standing behind a cloud of transparence, a pane of
    divine glass, an idea,
And appear to be laughing or whispering, but what can you hear?
    You prop your ladder in the black boughs

Of a cherry tree, which are like the legs of a swan, bark like a birch,
    pitch black—only birch and cherry
Have bark like that, like skin with sensual blemishes, both
    dusty and shiny. The women's soft bellies
Bulge as if each had swallowed a cat or been born with one
    growing inside them that forced its tail

From between their legs and curled it snugly against the bottoms
    of their stomachs, plus a paw
With tender pads half-hidden in fur. Your eyes blur with gratitude,
    and briefly, until you blink
Away your tears, the women are as featureless as bare feet
    or young girls pressed

Against that glass, cloud or idea. The petals of the cherry
    blossoms cover you with confetti.
You're like a bridegroom climbing your ridiculous ladder,
    reaching an arm in the air,
Running out of time, but getting nowhere, and the mind,
    that old adversary of desire,

Is no obstacle to women whispering nakedly, or to cats
　　and the pink pads
Of their complicated claws. There's nothing peculiarly Jewish
　　about this idea
Except the artist, who came from the Russian Ukraine and died
　　in Israel, God bless his heart.

SINGING THEIR HEARTS OUT

They couldn't sing, those sirens Odysseus ran into
Taxiing around the Aegean. Such interesting women,
    But their voices, ruined by cigarettes,
    Would shatter glass if they tried singing.
    Their talent was for laughing and crying
With noses deep in each other's bombshell hair,
    Squealing like bats in a cave. Their radar
Was their own half-nakedness and panic at attracting
    The wrong guy with wax in his ears,
    A stupid sailor, not an incognito king.
Experts at female doom, why heels are high, lips ruby,
    Hair big as dirigibles, on their island
Everyone was "Hon" or "Honey." Pretty as hawks,

Though a lot depends on the time of day, and always
    Complaining: inattentive husbands,
Not getting any younger, their mothers' insistence
    On grandchildren. But carry a tune? Never.
There they missed the idyllic boat they were always
    Humming about, trying a few tender notes,
Mis-remembering the words. And soon as they sense
The presence of men, their voices crack in an attack
    Of bad nerves, larynxes wracked from years
Of yearning and first-hand smoke. Yet certain men
    Aim their boats right at the rocks and the fog,
Again and again, trying to buy them whatever it is
    These beauties think for a minute they want.

The Internationale of Dogs

A haughty woman day after day passed an old dog on a street
    corner
And taunted him with a bone: "Jump, dummy!" In one hand
    she held the bone,
In the other a barbed wire whip, nine strands attached to the
    broomstick
Her grandmother used to ride, with which she gently caressed
    his haunches, his head,

Negligible red droplets that hardened into garnets the dog licked
    and scratched between visits.
It was a mongrel, part bloodhound, part St. Bernard, bloodhound
    in the face,
St. Bernard around the waist. Now he eyed the woman's white
    hollow bone,
Trembled and quivered. The instant he roused himself to jump,
    down came the whip.

Maybe the woman was a Nazi in recovery, with a houseful of
    lampshades and perfumed soap
To torment nostalgic memory. Occasionally she gave the poor
    dog a bone
And his still sometimes powerful jaws closed on it, crunching it,
    hoping for marrow.
Winter came. The river froze. The children trampled a path
    across the ice,

A shortcut to school. Suddenly there was a thaw. The ice broke, and the river roared,
Free from its season of chains, and some children were trapped on a rapidly melting ice island.
The old mongrel loped to the rescue, braving the raging ice waters and floes,
Bringing the children a rope, life jackets, and a little rum in a barrel he wore

Around his fat neck. He was old, the effort almost killed him, but he felt like a good dog.
The river froze again and in his doggy brain he realized the river was like the woman,
And if he wanted a lagoon he should live in Tahiti, or die and go to hell
Where it was at least warm, or go to heaven where every river made a waterfall,

A pool and a rainbow, where open-hearted brown-skinned women laughed and swam,
Likewise bestowing their gifts the way their island rivers flowed, freely and continuously.
Night fell on the dog's street-corner and the moon arose, cruel and elusive as the haughty woman,
And the dog began to moan: "Please whip me and feed me and let me come home!"

THE ALLIGATOR'S HUM

To allure an alligator lady so she'll allow him
To fertilize her eggs before she buries them
In her sand nest, the male alligator
      Hums in a swamp pond like a kid in a bathtub.
It hums like a foghorn: *Hummmmmm!* And raises
Queer geysers of water by his torso's profound
Vibrations, these inverted, fragile, almost crystal
Chandeliers his obligatto of amor. I have tried this
      On dates without knowing what I was doing:
Hummmmmm! My date pretended she didn't know
      What I was doing either and would ask,
"Are you all right?" *Hummmmmm!* I'd echo,

Something below my solar plexus now governing
My lowest, reptilian, ganglion brain. But I swear,
      Like people who claim they can't understand poetry,
She knew what it meant for the hum of the body
To dominate mind. It meant please admire
      My wet inverted chandeliers, which translates,
Like all of poetry too, into alligator: *"You can get me,*
      If you let me, you grinning, beautiful,
Primordial swampwater creature you!" Then their tails
      Slap the water with a belly whomp.
They thrash like mad, almost invisible—though the human
      Eye is never naked—and then it's over.

94

ACKNOWLEDGMENTS

Grateful acknowledgment is made to the editors of the following magazines where some of these poems first appeared: "Chairman Mao Swimming": *The Belgrade Circle*; "Crossing Brooklyn Ferry": *The Massachusetts Review;* "Persephone's Cave": *The Marlborough Review;* "The Origins of Tragedy": *Chelsea;* "The Woods in March": *Grand Street;* and "Thinking of Kissing You": *The Beloit Poetry Journal.*